Go, Tell It on the Mountain

Christmas Favorites for Solo Piano

arranged by **Lloyd Larson**

Moderately Easy

LILLENAS
PUBLISHING COMPANY

Lillenas.com

CONTENTS

Go, Tell It on the Mountain

Afro-American Spiritual
Arranged by Lloyd Larson

Steady ♩ = ca. 108

6

Silent Night! Holy Night!

FRANZ GRUBER
Arranged by Lloyd Larson

Tenderly ♩ = ca. 88

cresc.

mf

(opt. Cong. singing of Carol)

Hark! the Herald Angels Sing

FELIX MENDELSSOHN
Arranged by Lloyd Larson

Joyously ♩ = ca. 112

13

14

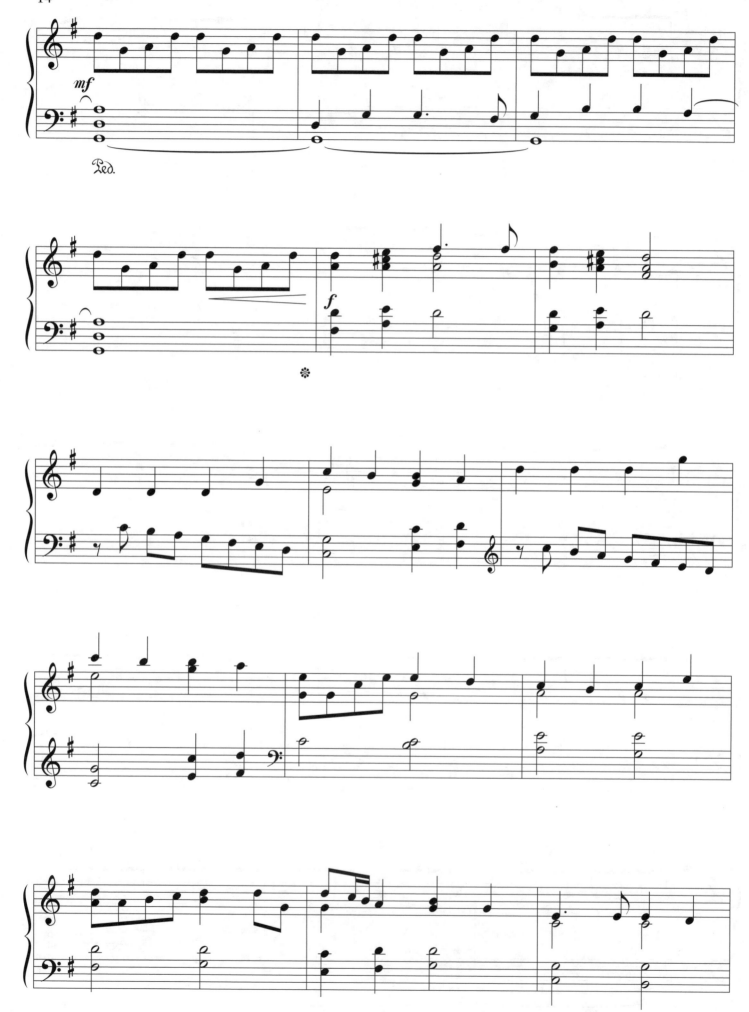

O Little Town of Bethlehem

LEWIS H. REDNER
Arranged by Lloyd Larson

Simply, freely ♩ = ca. 88

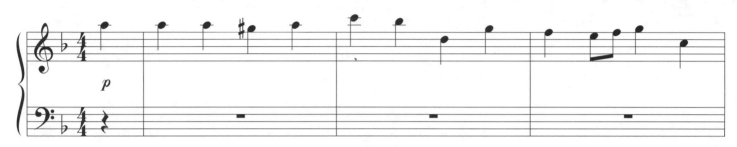

We Three Kings

JOHN H. HOPKINS, JR.
Arranged by Lloyd Larson

Gently, steady ♩ = ca. 144

cresc.

Once in Royal David's City

HENRY J. GAUNTLETT
Arranged by Lloyd Larson

Tenderly, freely ♩ = ca. 96

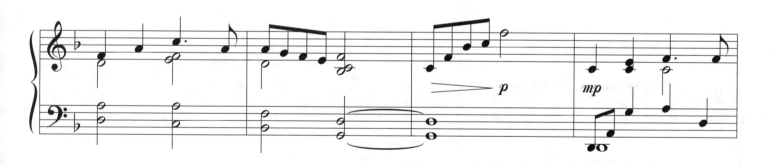

Joy to the World

GEORGE FREDERICK HANDEL
Arranged by Lloyd Larson

Joyously, lightly ♩ = ca. 104

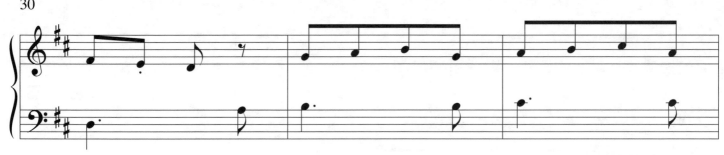

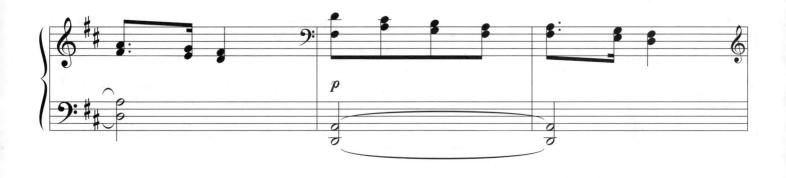

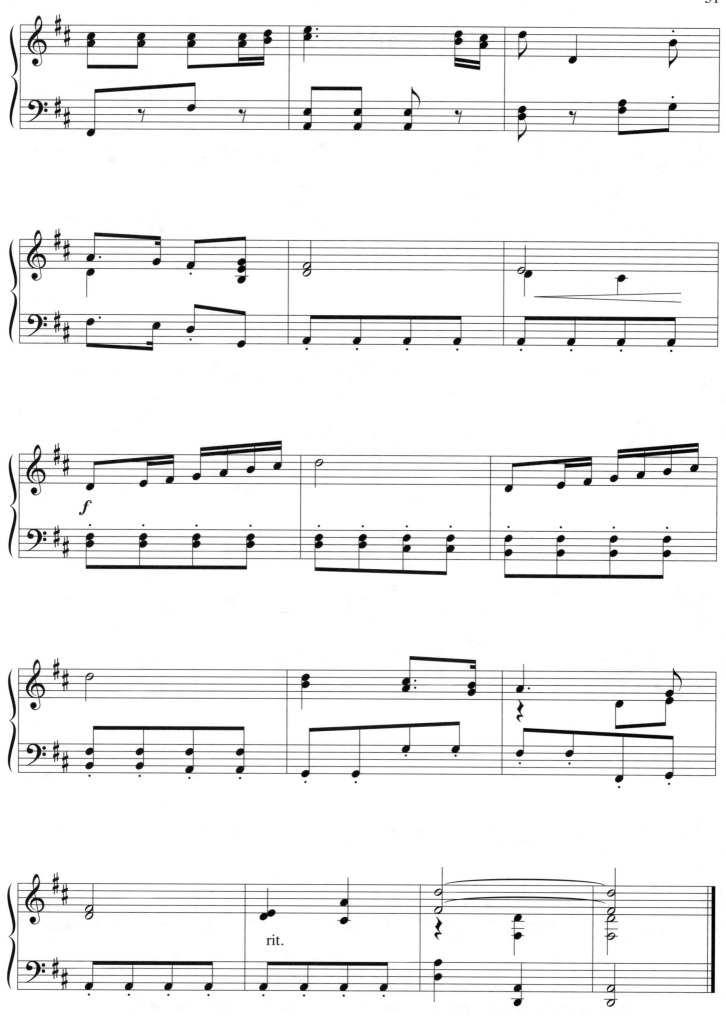

What Child Is This?

Traditional English Melody
Arranged by Lloyd Larson

With gentle, steady motion ♩ = ca. 132

34

O Come, All Ye Faithful

JOHN F. WADE
Arranged by Lloyd Larson

Regally ♩ = ca. 104

Broader ♩ = ca. 96

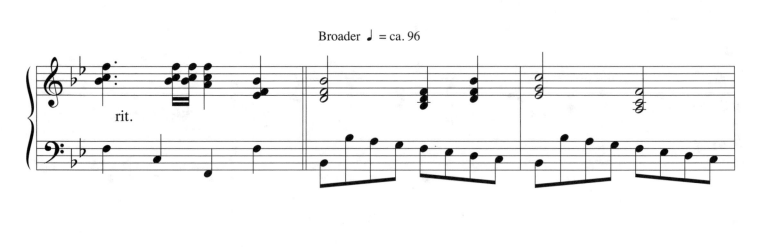

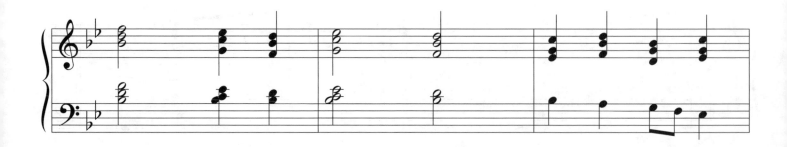

The First Noel

W. Sandy's *Christmas Carols*
Arranged by Lloyd Larson

Gently ♩ = ca. 100